SO
PROUDLY
THEY
SERVED

WAAC

THIS IS MY WAR TOO!
WOMEN'S ARMY AUXILIARY CORPS
UNITED · STATES · ARMY

SO PROUDLY THEY SERVED

AMERICAN MILITARY WOMEN IN WORLD WAR II

BY MADELYN KLEIN ANDERSON

A First Book
Franklin Watts
New York / Chicago / London / Toronto / Sydney

Cover art by Jane Sterrett

Photographs copyright ©: Women's Army Corps Museum: pp. 2, 18, 21, 26, 33, 36, 40, 45, 50; The Bettmann Archive: p. 10; Women in Military Service for America Memorial Foundation, Inc.: pp. 11, 12, 15, 31, 57; Library of Congress: p. 14; American Red Cross: p. 16; National Archives: pp. 22, 24, 32, 42; Photofest: p. 28; U.S. Coast Guard: p. 38; Iva Lee Holtz Collection, Admiral Nimitz Museum: p. 47; American Legion Auxilliary: p. 52; UPI/Bettmann: p. 56; Herald Tribune/Rice: p. 58.

Library of Congress Cataloging-in-Publication Data

Anderson, Madelyn Klein.
    So proudly they served : American military women in World War II / by Madelyn Klein Anderson.
        p. cm. — (A First book)
        Includes bibliographical references and index.
        ISBN 0-531-20197-X (lib. bdg.)
            1. United States—Armed Forces—Women—History—Juvenile literature.
    2. Women and the military—United States—History—Juvenile literature.
    3. World War, 1939-1945—Women—Juvenile literature. [1. United States—Armed Forces—Women—History. 2. Women and the military History.]
        I. Title. II. Series.
UB418.W65A53 1995
940.54'0973—dc20   94-39907
                                                                CIP
                                                                AC

ACKNOWLEDGMENTS

I am grateful to Brig. Gen. Wilma L. Vaught, USAF (Ret.), president of the Women in Military Service for America Memorial Foundation, Inc. (WIMSA), for critiquing the manuscript; Mrs. Irma Kramer, of the office of Congressman Charles E. Schumer, for assistance in procuring research materials from the Library of Congress; and Ms. Minna Kirman of the Navy Office of Information in New York City and Ms. Cecille Jach of the American Occupational Therapy Association Archives for supplying answers to my questions. Thanks are also due the editor, E. Russell Primm III, for his expertise and support. Thank you all.

CONTENTS

PRELUDE

It was 1869. The War Between the States was dividing and devastating the United States of America. Loreta Velasques watched her husband go off to fight—and to die—and knew that she had do something more than sit at home and mourn. So she cut off her hair and fashioned it into a mustache and beard, put on a uniform over a tight binding that flattened out her womanly hips and bosom, recruited a mounted troop of men, and went to war as Lt. Harry T. Buford. Wounded, she was found out and booted out, but re-enlisted as an ordinary foot soldier. It didn't take her long to realize she preferred the privileges of rank, so she fashioned herself once again into a cavalry officer. Once again she was badly wounded and unmasked, and finally gave up going to war.

Loreta Velasques made a convincing Lt. Harry T. Buford.

In 1776, in the American Revolution, a few women disguised themselves as men, but most went to war openly. In those days, and for hundreds of years before then in Europe, women were allowed to follow husbands, sons, and fathers to the battlefield. Called "Daughters of the Regiment" and "camp followers" (a term used today only for prostitutes, who also followed early armies), these women could not survive at home without their men to provide for them. The Army fed them and sometimes gave them a small stipend for their services, and that was good enough. These women marched with the Army from battlefield to battlefield. They cooked and washed clothes and tended to the wounded and helped load muskets and cannons. Many used those guns when there was a threat of being overrun or their men had been killed or wounded. But then we don't know how many women bore arms in the American Revolution. We don't know how many men fought, either. Few records were

Deborah Sampson disguised herself as a man and fought in the American Revolution. She was shot but nursed herself so that her true identity would not be revealed. She lived to tell about it—this portrait of her was done in 1797.

kept, and the Army was disbanded at the end of the war.

When the War of 1812 erupted, the new United States of America did not have much of an Army. The government had kept a standing Army of only eighty men, because no one had envisioned another war. Men were desperately needed to fight, and an unknown number of women decided to disguise themselves and fight alongside them. One of these women was Lucy Brewer, who made herself into George Baker, a marine. Somehow, she managed to serve for three years aboard the USS *Constitution*. Serving aboard a crowded battleship in disguise must have been harder to pull off than being in the Army with lots of land around for privacy. Civil War wooded encampments offered more seclusion . It wasn't even necessary for a woman to use a fake mustache and beard to disguise herself as Loreta Velasques did. Boys as young as eleven and twelve were being enlisted on both sides, and it wasn't hard for a young woman to pass as a boy who had not yet begun to shave. Recruiters did not look too closely at desperately needed volunteers. Neither did the troops, until a wound or some sickness would give a woman's identity away. One supposed male Confederate soldier gave birth in a Yankee prison camp! And a number of women served openly as women when they were swept up in the fighting on their farms and in their villages.

Historians think about four hundred women fought in the Civil War. Only a few are known by name. Many went to their graves as men.

Some women who ran hospitals

Dr. Mary Walker, physician and only woman to hold the Congressional Medal of Honor. She was also an early suffragette who advocated "sensible" clothing for women, such as this forerunner of today's pantsuit.

were commissioned as captains in the Confederate Army. In the Union Army, Dr. Mary Walker, a physician who at first was only allowed to practice as a nurse, was finally sworn in as a lieutenant and served as an assistant surgeon—and sometimes as a spy. She was awarded the Congressional Medal of Honor. (The award was taken away from her and many other recipients when, in World War I, it was decided to bestow the medal as the country's highest honor for exceptional bravery. But a special act of Congress restored Dr. Walker's award in 1976.)

Women on both sides of the Civil War were recruited to assist the military in the dangerous jobs of saboteurs and spies—a hanging offense if captured. Probably the best known of these is Harriet Tubman, an escaped slave who put the Underground Railroad to use for covert activities just as she had used it to smuggle slaves to freedom before the war.

While women on both sides worked to establish sanitary conditions in hospitals, nursing itself was considered unseemly for respectable women, unless they were related to the patient. It was thought to be embarrassing to the men to have strange women tend them. But when casualties and illnesses mounted, that changed. The Union government finally issued a call for "very plain" women to act as civilian nurses. These women had to dress in all-black or dark brown plain dresses and be over the age of thirty, so they would not be attractive to men. The work was terrible and unceasing, and at war's end, the women were sent home to uncertain futures by an uncaring government.

In 1898, when the Spanish-American War broke out

Harriet Tubman, freedom
fighter and Civil War spy

and typhoid and yellow fever raged in military camps, the Army tried to enlist six thousand men as nurses. That did not work out too well, and once again the country turned to its women to act as civilian nurses.

In 1901, not wanting ever again to be without nursing care for the country's fighting men, Congress authorized the creation of an all-female Nurse Corps Division as an auxiliary to the Army. In 1908, the Navy got its own Nurse Corps, which also served the Coast Guard and the Marines. The military would not go so far as to give the nurses military rank and benefits, but the Nurse Corps offered job security and a place for those who felt the need to serve their country.

In 1917, when the United States entered World War I, the Army and Navy Nurse Corps were in place to care for casualties. And an estimated fifteen thousand

Clara Maas, a nurse in the Spanish-American War, allowed herself to be bitten by the mosquitoes suspected of carrying yellow fever. The experiment proved fatal to her, but saved countless thousands of lives.

American women, all civilians, volunteered their services overseas to help the military. Many paid their own expenses, and others were members of volunteer service organizations such as the Red Cross. Still others were civilians called "reconstruction aides"—occupational and physical therapists, recreation specialists, and dietitians—who were listed on the government payroll as cleaning women because there was no other category in which they fit in order to be paid.

But no one had to disguise herself to take on active part in the war. About thirty-four thousand women served in the military in World War I not only in the Nurse Corps or on reserve status as physicians, but as sailors and marines. They could not serve in the Army, because Congress had restricted its ranks by law to men only. But the law governing recruitment for the Navy and Marines did not differentiate between men and women. It simply called for "citizens." When the law had been written, nobody had even considered that "citizens" might include women. But in 1917 the secretary of the navy, Josephus Daniels, needed personnel to do the paperwork that was keeping men on desk duty rather than at sea, and he took

A World War I nurse at a field hospital close to the front lines in France. The men on the stretchers have been blinded by poison gas— one of the great horrors of that war.

Yeomen (F) or "Yeomenettes" in
World War I, part of a select group

advantage of the wording of the law. So women became "yeomen (F)" and "marines (F)." "F" meant female, of course, and "yeomen" was the name the Navy used for its enlisted men on desk duty rather than its combat-ready "seamen." While Navy women soon became "yeomenettes" because it was easier to say, understandably the term "marinettes" was discouraged in the Marines!

In 1925, the law for recruiting "citizens" into the Navy was changed to read "male citizens," and the yeomen (F) and marines (F) were history. When they were mustered out, they were not given medical benefits or pensions that male veterans received. They were barely thanked. Only the nurses, considered a necessary evil, were allowed to stay in the military. Other service-women were seen as a threat to men, who were having trouble hanging on to their niches in the rapidly shrinking military of peacetime. People were convinced there would be no more war—World War I had been called "the war to end all wars." Many were pacifists who not only were not interested in women's right to retain their jobs but who wanted the military to disband altogether. Others were isolationists who believed that this country should not be involved in other countries' affairs.

Unfortunately, the United States had long since grown too important to isolate itself from the rest of the world. And only twenty-one years after the armistice of World War I, the world erupted in World War II.

2 "MOTHER'S A MARINE, SIS A SOLDIER"

It was 1939. Japan was at war with China and Korea. Germany was effortlessly swallowing up the countries of middle Europe. Great Britain threatened to declare war if the Nazis invaded Poland. German forces marched into Poland on September 3, and Europe was engulfed in World War II. The United States of America stood back and watched and then readied itself for the day when it would be drawn into war, a day which seemed inevitable despite pacifist and isolationist pressures.

A draft of young men went into effect in the United States in September 1940. Any question of a draft of women was quickly dismissed. But several plans had been advanced for women to serve with—not in—the Army. In May 1941, Congresswoman Edith Nourse

Congresswoman Edith Nourse Rogers,
whose bill to establish a Women's Auxiliary
Army Corps finally passed Congress

The Japanese bombardment of Pearl Harbor and the
start of American involvement in World War II

Rogers introduced a bill to establish such a parallel military unit, the Women's Auxiliary Army Corps, or WAAC. Women of high moral character and good education and skills were to be recruited to work at menial jobs considered a waste of men's abilities, even though men were not required to have women's high qualifications. Some members of Congress reacted with horror to the idea of women in the Army. One Representative said, "Take the women into the armed service, who then will do the cooking, the washing, the mending, the humble homey tasks to which every woman has devoted herself. Think of the humiliation! What has become of the manhood of America?"

Against this kind of opposition, it would take a full year to get the WAAC bill passed into law. During that year, the inevitable day came when the United States was finally drawn into World War II: December 7, 1941— Pearl Harbor Day. On December 8, war was declared on Japan, three days later the United States was at war with Germany as well.

The United States faced a war on two sides of the world. While the enlistment rate was high in the days after Pearl Harbor, and the draft was stepped up, the Army was short by an estimated 160,000 men. Again there was talk, more serious talk this time, of drafting women. Great Britain's conscription of women had begun after the Japanese offensive against her in the Pacific, and it had proven very successful. Rather than subject American women to a draft, however, Congresswoman Rogers's bill establishing the voluntary WAAC was finally

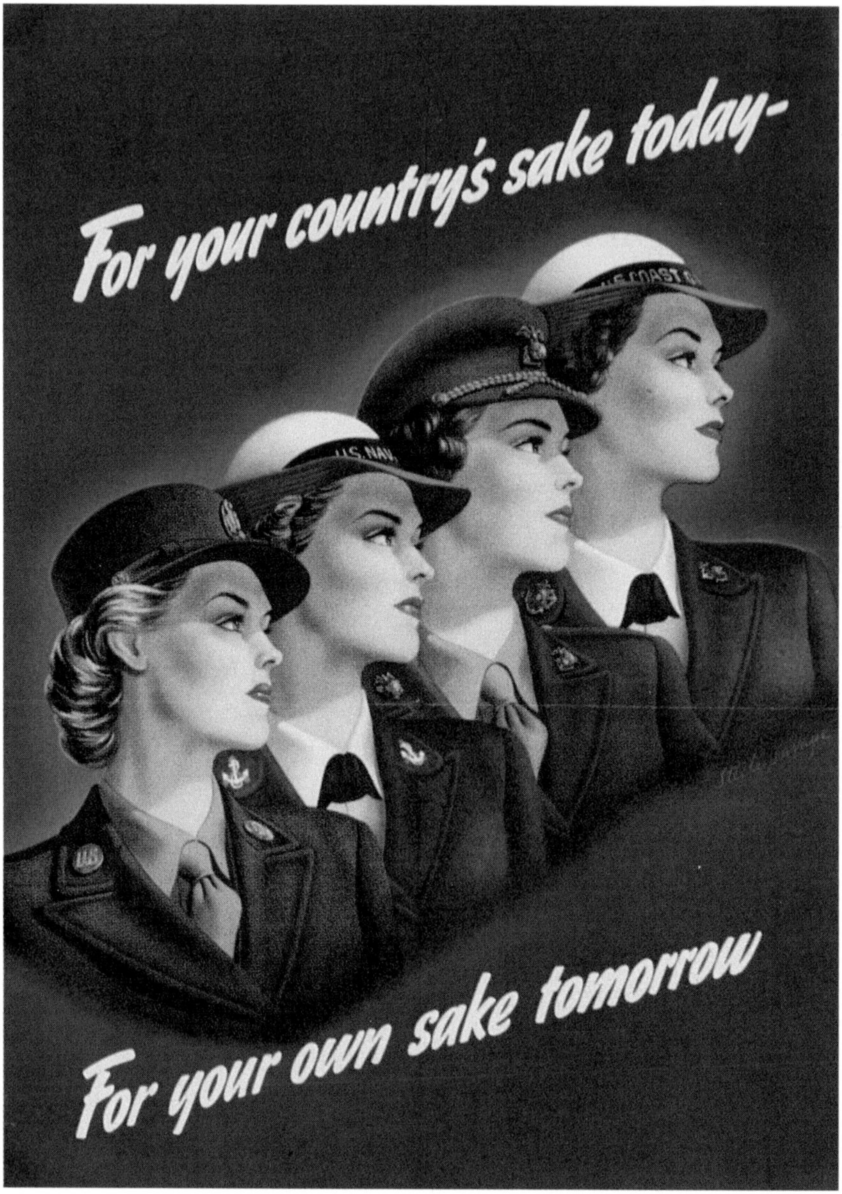
For your country's sake today-
For your own sake tomorrow

passed by Congress in May 1942. In July of that year, another bill established the Navy Women's Reserve (which covered the Marines as well), and in November, the Coast Guard Women's Reserve. Once again, the women marines were called simply "marines," but with no "F" tagged on. A snappy title for Navy women was wanted—and wanted urgently after a newspaper nick-named them "Gobletts." They became WAVES, for "Women Accepted for Voluntary Emergency Service," although some jokers were soon saying it meant "Women Are Very Essential Sometimes." The Coast Guard called women SPARs, from the Coast Guard motto *"Semper Paratus"* ("Always Ready") and drawing on the fact that spars are sturdy poles forming masts and booms and other vital parts of sailing ships. (Women in the Air Force, or WAF, were not part of World War II. The WAF was created in July 1947, at the same time as the Air Force.)

Women's uniforms as well as their names became front-page news. WAAC uniforms were not the prettiest, were made of scratchy wool, and had been designed on models of men with little regard for the realities of women's shapes—but they had military zing. WAVE uni-forms were prettier, more comfortable, and were de-signed by one of the great dress designers of all time, Mainbocher. The uniform was sometimes a factor when

The country was flooded with
recruiting posters like this one.

Work uniforms: winter wear on a SPAR, far left,
and summer wear on a Marine, WAC, and WAVE.

a woman was deciding which branch of service she
wanted to enter, and recruiters emphasized it. (This was
not a feminine foible; a lot of men chose to enter the
Army rather than wear a sailor suit or went into the
Marines because the uniform was so attractive.) Women

were allowed to carry a government-issued (GI) pocket-book. Papers and books needed for work could be carried while on duty, but officers could carry nothing else at any time unless it fit into the pocketbook. Umbrellas were not GI and could not be carried under any circumstances! Everything about the women was debated, down to the color and material of their underwear and stockings. An admiral who was set on WAVES wearing then-unfashionable black stockings they didn't want allowed manufacturers to go ahead with a neutral color only when told that black dye contained an ingredient that was essential for gunpowder and was in short supply!

It took another debate and an official decision that women officers be recognized as women and called "ma'am" rather than "sir." (This seems to be obvious, but consider that fifty years later the television series "Star Trek: The Next Generation" chose to have its female officers addressed as "sir," as though all command functions had to be masculine. All women's units were commanded by "ma'ams," although the top females had male commanders over them, up to President Franklin Delano Roosevelt. (Mrs. Roosevelt, however, sometimes exerted her influence over the men making decisions for the women!)

WAACs served with the Army but were not in it, while WAVES, SPARs, and women marines were "in" their service. WAACs, therefore, were not entitled to extra pay, allowances for dependents, or veteran's benefits, while other servicewomen were. WAACs did not even have a legal, set enlistment term and could leave

The crew of "Star Trek: The Next Generation."
Obviously, not all of them are "sirs." You wonder
how Lt. Worf would accept being called "ma'am."

whenever they wanted, although many were not made aware of that fact. The Army found that maintaining control over such an auxiliary force was difficult. Getting the women to where they were most needed and deciding which units had the greater need, who had authority over whom, providing supplies, coordinating commands, and so on, proved more of a problem than acknowledging that the women were soldiers.

It was decided to bring WAACs into the Army. In 1943, the WAAC became the WAC, the Women's Army Corps. Hardly anyone outside the military noticed. The WACs did, however, because now they were entitled to the same ranks (only up to major at the time) and therefore the same pay schedules as the men. WAACs who did not want to make the move did not have to, and several thousand left military service—without veteran's benefits. Not until many years later did Congress pass a law giving former WAACs such benefits.

WACs were not the only women in the Army nor WAVES the only women in the Navy. The Army Nurse Corps and the Navy Nurse Corps had been operational since World War I. Also as in World War I, female physicians and dentists (there were two) served as reservists on home front duty, and while they wore WAC or WAVES uniforms, they had no other connection to these units.

Other women served the military but were not officially part of it. Physical therapists and dietitians were civil service employees in the Army Medical Department until 1943, when they were made military officers. Occupational therapists stayed in the Army Medical Department as civilians throughout the war. Two other civilian groups of women, the Women's Auxiliary Ferrying Squadron, or WAFS, and the Women's Air Force Service Pilots, or WASPs, were organized along military lines. They later combined into one unit, the WASPs. These women flew every kind of plane the military had. They trained some of those men to fly. They ferried planes to air bases around the world so that men could fly them into combat. They flew planes that had been discarded as unfit for combat but usable to tow targets for inexperienced gunners to practice shooting at. More than sixty of them were killed in their jobs, but because they were not military, even burial expenses were not available for them. Sometimes a collection had to be taken up to raise the money for a funeral for a woman killed in a craft. The WASPs were disbanded in December 1944, and it was not until 1977 that their contributions were recognized: they were made part of the military retroactively. This gave them veteran's benefits and also the status due them—the country's first military women pilots.

By the end of the war, more than 400,000 women had served in the WAAC/WAC, the Army Nurse Corps, and the Navy Nurse Corps, the WAVES, the SPARs, the Marines. The women did far more than the menial jobs projected for them when these units were organized. They became skilled technicians, radio and telephone operators, flight instructors, parachute packers, mail clerks, mechanics, navigation specialists, air traffic controllers, truck drivers, typists, and on and on. Calls for their services in all kinds of jobs poured in, as military com-

A WASP at work

manders realized that women could do a lot more than housework. It was estimated that in the WAC alone, one million women were needed. (But the WAC numbered only about one hundred thousand at its peak.) As the war went on, women enlisted in fewer numbers. The shortage of nurses was so bad that free schooling was offered

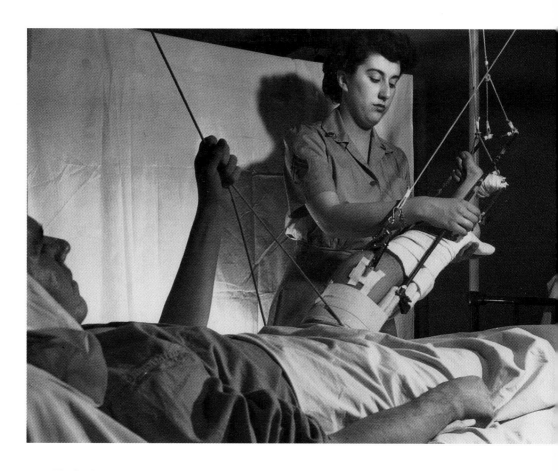

To help overcome the desperate shortage of nurses, a new career field was created: medical technician. This Army technician is adjusting traction equipment, not a task requiring a registered nurse.

WAVES repair the propeller of a fighter. Women never did this kind of work before the war—or lots of other kinds, either.

to those willing to serve as nurses, and a bill to draft nurses almost became law. It was passed by the House of Representatives, but before the Senate could act on it, the war had ended. It was not that women had lost their sense of patriotism or their desire to do something for the war effort. It was not that the women were not badly needed or wanted or that their role in helping the war effort was not recognized. Albert Speer, the Nazi in charge of German war production, was to say that if his country had mobilized its women as Americans had, it would have won the war. But many unexpected issues were keeping women from enlisting in the military, issues that even today have not been entirely solved.

3 SNAFUS AND SLANDERS

It was 1943. Rosie the Riveter, the symbol of women workers in war production factories, had become the country's darling, a heroine. Rosie the WAC, WAVE, SPAR, marine was regarded by many Americans as immoral. Women in military roles were seen by many men—and women, too—as a threat to the entire social structure of the country.

This had not been in women's minds in the first rush to enlist. The same patriotic fervor beat in their hearts as in Loreta Velasques's. Women in Great Britain's military were much admired, and no one had thought that American women would not be just as highly regarded. But here, the war was less of a reality. There were no air raids killing women and men and children indiscriminately. The privations were not so great, the casualties

British military women work
with two American WACs.

were not so visible, the need was not so apparent. And as more and more men went off to fight, there was resentment that the safe jobs that many men hoped to get when they were drafted were being given to women instead. It was not that the men—most of them little more than boys—were not brave. They simply wanted to survive, and their families wanted them to survive. Women taking over noncombatant jobs meant more men free to fight. This was the military's aim in recruiting women, and many men saw it as a threat to their very lives. Many mothers, wives, and girlfriends saw it the same way. Women in civilian jobs bringing men the equipment and supplies they needed was one thing; freeing men up to become cannon fodder was another. Wives at home also feared that husbands working together with military women far from home could form relationships that would break up their marriage. Such resentments and fears found outlets in hate and smear campaigns, and military women and WASPs were defamed and harassed.

Although women enlistees had to present proof of high moral character from teachers, physicians, or religious leaders and other professionals, and men were not asked for such proof, rumors about women's characters were rampant. The women were slandered as camp followers recruited for use by the troops, as Germany and Japan were doing with women from conquered countries. Or, if they weren't actual prostitutes, they were easy sexual conquests. Or, they had enlisted only to find husbands for their allotments. Or they were of poor char-

acter, mentally unstable, inefficient and incapable, demanding and in need of constant coddling. Or they were all lesbians. The bad-mouthing was endless.

Although often not believed, slanders planted suspicion and reservations in the public's mind, and in the military's. It got so bad that an enemy plot was suspected. First Lady Eleanor Roosevelt blamed Nazi propaganda. Finally, Army intelligence agents and the FBI investigated and discovered the culprits to be men of the U.S. military, including officers. The men were circulating dirty jokes and cartoons and writing anonymous letters for publication in military post newspapers all over the country. Civilian grapevines soon took up the refrain. It is a wonder that any women enlisted at all in the face of these attitudes. Yes, some of them were looking for husbands, and some were lesbians, and some met men they loved, but that had nothing to do with their desire to serve their country. Rather it was their need to be part of the action, up there on the stage and not behind the scenes. They didn't want to be men, but they wanted to do as much as men were doing for their country.

Some were mothers, wives, sisters, and daughters of men who were fighting or had been killed or made prisoner and they felt the need to do something to show their

This SPAR, a trainee at the U.S. Coast Guard Academy, is the mother of a Congressional Medal of Honor Coast Guardsman killed in the Pacific.

WAACS FIGHT BACK

'Sinister Rumors, Aimed at Destroying Their Reputation' Are Denounced

By ELEANOR DARNTON

WASHINGTON.

THE morals of the Women's Army Auxiliary Corps have been examined in the brutal light of national publicity and have been found good. There seems little likelihood that there will be a Congressional investigation of the rumors of immorality would interfere with recruiting for the corps or destroy its reputation interfered with the combat strength of the Army, and so was of value to the enemy.

Waac officers say it is too early to tell whether the maligning of the corps has had any effect on recruiting throughout the country

Rumors and slander about military women led to a congressional investigation and newspaper articles.

solidarity with their loved ones. Others were looking for more exciting, interesting lives and work than they could find in traditional female roles. Many wanted to travel, to live in cities, to go overseas. Many found to their chagrin that they were sent to isolated posts or held humdrum jobs. The WAVES paraphrased the men's ditty, "We joined the Navy to see the world, and what did we see? We saw the sea," to ". . . what did we see? We saw D.C."

Undoubtedly, the women who were shot at and torpedoed and the sixty-six Army nurses and eleven Navy nurses made prisoners of war after the battles of Corregidor and Bataan would have been glad to spend their enlistments in Washington, D.C. Instead, except for a few of them who were exchanged, they spent the entire war in detention camps under conditions of great deprivation, particularly as the Japanese ran short of medical and food supplies and diverted them to their armies.

American military women and women attached to the military served in every theater of operations around the world. Again, the total number serving overseas for all the years of the war is vague, but the number peaked at about 17,000. They were nurses, aides, secretaries, drivers, clerks, telephone and radio operators, cooks, dietitians, therapists, and more. One battalion of WACs was sent to Europe to deal with the mail, whose delivery had turned into a serious problem. The mails were the only link between those serving overseas and their home, and letters and packages were all-important to morale. The unit was composed of black women, and while they got on very well in England, American bigots circulated the same vicious rumors of their really being sent abroad to be used as prostitutes by black troops, just as white military women were said to be for the use of white troops. Women who had believed their country would regard them as heroines found themselves demeaned instead.

Serving in the military was difficult for black women in World War II. The Army had a quota for blacks of 10 percent, the same percentage as there were blacks in the

general population. While this was meant in part to quiet fears that any particular group in society would bear more than its share of military service, it was also quota prejudice. Black women looked for other ways to serve their country. The Army fell far short of its quota for black women, who numbered in all only about four thousand, or 1 percent of the total WAC strength. (The Navy did not recruit black women at all until almost the end of the war. The Marines did not bring in black women or men until 1948, when all the military services were desegregated.)

Most black military women found themselves segregated. Even those who did not serve in segregated units often found themselves in uncomfortable situations, particularly socially. Although the Army tried not to station black women near towns and cities where color prejudice was active, this could not always be avoided. Going off base to a restaurant or movie in such places could cause problems or embarrassment. On base, a black woman in a mostly white unit could be very lonely, because even the most casual mixed-race dating was taboo. So some black women found themselves in the position of requesting duty in northern cities where segregation was not practiced but in segregated units where they would be less lonely!

There weren't enough numbers of racially or ethnically

Black military women served in segregated units.

distinct women to create other segregated units, although two hundred Japanese-American (Nisei) women were recruited to serve as an intelligence unit. While there were many Jewish women who enlisted, they were not always identified as such. Many falsified their religious identity so they would not be discriminated against—the military was as anti-Semitic as anti-black.

Military women were segregated also by sex and rank. Women lived in segregated quarters that allowed men in a designated public area only—perhaps a porch or anteroom. Women officers did not socialize with enlisted women. And it was an unwritten but enforced rule that women officers did not date enlisted men. This was almost the very first thing that a woman officer was taught upon entering the service. During the war, uniforms had to be worn at all times, so officers and enlisted personnel were easily distinguishable. Getting far enough away from a post was virtually impossible; cars and taxis were few, gasoline was rationed, rubber tires were worth their weight in gold. Even relatives could not socialize in a public place if one was an officer and the other an enlisted person. One WAC enlisted woman requested written permission to have dinner in a restaurant with her father, a general, without being hassled by military police. The event went down in military history. The crossing of barriers between ranks was seen as a breakdown in discipline, a show of favoritism by an officer for an enlisted person that other enlisted persons would resent, or a violation of each other's turf. Black women officers in Europe had a particularly hard time socially, because black male

Segregated black women officers had a particularly lonely time in Europe as there were few black male officers. Women, no matter what race, were not allowed to associate with enlisted personnel.

officers were almost nonexistent (black male units had white male officers) and interracial dating was taboo in the American armed forces. Although the rules against fraternization were put in writing only by the Army, all the services saw to it that they were obeyed. Those who disobeyed were punished swiftly, and in the case of male-female involvement, it was usually the female who was punished.

Under these circumstances, marriages between an enlisted person and an officer were extremely rare and had to be kept secret. If discovered, husband and wife would be discharged (a situation that existed until the 1980s). Even a marriage that did not cross the officer-enlisted barrier was discouraged, and punished by transfer to separate duty stations. Pregnancy meant immediate discharge, whether the woman was married or not. And the discovery of lesbian activity could mean psychiatric hospitalization and discharge. Discharge was a more common punishment for women than men, because the process was easier for women volunteers than male draftees.

There was segregation, discrimination, and harassment on many fronts. But the military has never been a democratic institution, particularly during a war. The military was responsible for millions of people and did not want to be bothered with all the complicated issues of personal freedom and relationships and thought strict policing would put a stop to it all. Because military personnel were not robots, personal issues and their complications occurred, and the military bumbled along in its

Far from leading a life of glamour and play, this officer is doing what every woman had to do in the military—spend hours every night on laundering uniforms and shining shoes.

efforts to deal with them. As the military was—and is—fond of saying, it was a snafu, "situation normal, all fouled up."

It made a lot of sense for women to keep their personal freedom by taking civilian jobs that paid more, let them stay at home (if that was what they wanted), and were just as patriotic—if not as glamorous. As the war intensified, more women opted to be Rosie the Riveter rather than Private Rosie. They did not want to be left at war's end with a tarnished reputation for having served in the military. A number of women veterans of World War II tell of how they were looked at as "fallen women." They laugh, but the pain is there. In actuality, these women were pioneers in the fight for equality between the sexes and against ethnic and racial discriminatory practices. They just didn't know it—they saw themselves as part of a war with a different cause, a killing war, not an ideological one.

4

WOMEN ARE VETERANS, TOO!

It was 1945. World War II was finally over. Military women were ready to go home, but their term of service was for "the duration of the emergency plus six months," not the duration of the war. The need to get millions of men back from overseas and to their home areas for demobilizing constituted a real emergency, as did putting armies of occupation in place. The women were experts at handling administrative and clerical details, and the military wasn't going to let them go too quickly.

Many of the women were just as eager as the men to get back to homes and loved ones and normalize their lives or get a job before the returning male veterans got them all. Few of them were interested in fighting for a permanent place in a peacetime military, for equal rights

WAC clerk at the European Air Transport
Service headquarters helps with the awesome
task of moving millions of occupation troops
into and out of Europe.

with men in the military. Historians find that a mystery, but these military women had already fought quite a fight. They had overcome disapproval and slander and prejudice to prove they were men's equals in every area of the military they were allowed to enter. That they did very little to capitalize on this, to continue the fight for women's equality, is not so mysterious. They had been interested in fighting a war, not a revolution. They had come through that war and were ready to take the place that society always offered them as wives and mothers. They were barraged with propaganda about a woman's place being in the home, comforting and assisting men who were returning from battle. Even their leaders did not see a place for women in the permanent military, except for nurses. And if their leaders did not fight for their jobs, how could the women do so?

But General Eisenhower and a few other male top brass were doing their utmost to keep women troops in the other services as long as possible. Full military status was given nurses in April 1947, although it was to take a year more of heated debate before Congress passed the Women's Armed Services Integration Act that opened the peacetime military to women. Now, women could make a career in three Nurse Corps (Army, Navy, and Air Force), WAC, WAVES, WAF, Marines, and in the Coast Guard. In 1949, the Army and the Air Force each organized an all-officer Women's Medical Specialist Corps, or WMSC, consisting of occupational therapists, physical therapists, and dietitians. Not until the late 1970s and early 1980s did the last female unit designations, or acronyms, disappear,

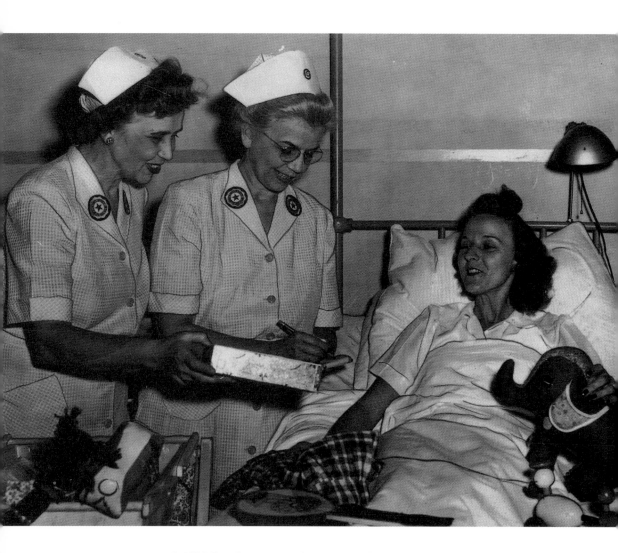

A WAC who served in New Guinea and the
Philippines is seen recuperating from disabilities
in a VA hospital, where she is cheered by
American Legion Auxiliary Volunteers.

and all women became simply servicewomen—not WACs or WAVES, or WAFs.

Women who chose to leave the services after the war became part of the ocean of veterans in a world of civilians, but, unlike the men, most of them did not profit from being veterans. They simply were not recognized. They rarely were given veterans' preference in hiring. Women who wanted to join veterans' organizations, such as the American Legion, found that they were not wanted. They could join only the women's auxiliary meant for wives and daughters of male veterans, women who had never been in the military but were there as volunteers, for drives to raise funds or to provide coffee and cookies at the end of meetings. Ex-servicewomen's concerns had no forum for expression.

The Department of Veterans Affairs (VA), the vast organization created to deal with issues of veterans' health and welfare, was male-run and male-centered. Women veterans seeking assistance often found themselves treated as strange intruders. Vocational and resettlement guidance was difficult to get, VA-insured home mortgages did not seem to be available to them. VA hospitals were essentially closed to them. By regulation, women could be admitted only if they had service-connected disabilities. Because relatively few of them had been wounded or injured, and hospitals were overcrowded, this made sense at first. But when beds became available, and men were accommodated even if their problem was not service-connected, women were still not admitted. Even those with a service-connected disability were sent elsewhere for help on the excuse that no facilities—wards or bathrooms—were available for them. The rare female admission usually had to endure the discomfort of a potty chair by her bed, simply because no one wanted to be bothered to set up a toilet facility.

No one knows how many women asked for the educational and other benefits to which they were entitled as veterans covered by the GI Bill of Rights and the Servicemen's Readjustment Act of 1944, which was designed "to make up for time and opportunities lost." Nobody kept data on the women, who represented less than 2 percent of the veteran population. This was considered too small a number to keep statistics on. The U.S. Census Bureau did not even bother to ask women whether they had been in the military until 1980, thirty-five years after the war had ended.

Some of this lack of sensitivity to women veterans was simply unthinking, but much of it was conscious discrimination to keep women "in their place," and that place was in the home. It could not have been more effective. Many women veterans found that they were more comfortable if they ignored their military past. Those who today say that these World War II women should have battled harder for equal rights are not aware of how hard they did fight. They just didn't win at first. Nor do they realize that military women in World War II did not see their rights as equal to men's. They had been strongly disciplined to accept men's superior roles. After the war, men wanted to pick up their lives as they were before the war, and that meant having their women back in traditional roles. And that's what many women were ready to do. Others who wanted jobs and equal pay found that male employers were not as eager to help women veterans—they were leery of their self-assurance, their knowledge, and their assumption of equal rights. Most women veterans had all they could do to fight for themselves in civilian life, much less fight for the rights of all women. Those who did, soon found they had to spend their energies fighting the rising tide of antimilitary sentiments of the Korean War.

Gradually, however, World War II women became more active in veterans' affairs, particularly as women from later wars joined them. They started their own support organizations and their own American Legion posts—equal, but not together. Today, in Washington, D.C., an organization of women veterans and women in the armed forces is seeking to honor all American military women, from the Revolution's Daughters of the Regiment to World War II veterans to today's carrier pilots and mission specialists. The Women in Military Service for America Memorial Foundation, Inc. (WIMSA), is attempting to find all the women who served in the military over the history of our country. Records for women veterans of World War II are almost as incomplete as they are for World War I. (For that matter, it is difficult to find out how many women served in the Korean and Vietnam wars.) One of WIMSA's main efforts is directed at getting the more than one million living women veterans to identify themselves. Sadly, some women are still reluctant to be publicly named as honored members of the military. It is possible that they are embarrassed by the slanders that have not disappeared over the years. Or they may be apprehensive

The three heads of the women's uniformed services: (from left) Lt. Comdr. Mildred M. McAfee of the WAVES, Colonel Oveta Culp Hobby of the WACs, and Lt. Comdr. Dorothy Stratton of the SPARs.

of antimilitary displays by those who choose to ignore the fact that the military fights only when governments do not keep the peace, and that the military is one of the greatest voices for peace we have.

Despite their poor reception from the public, almost

The Women in Military Service for America Memorial will be built at the gateway to Arlington National Cemetery.

all women veterans of World War II—or any other period—feel in their hearts a great pride for their military service. These women dedicated themselves to their country in a time of need, and it is time for their country to recognize and honor them.

FOR FURTHER READING

Anticaglia, Elizabeth. *Heroines of '76*. New York: Walker, 1975.

Ayer, Eleanor H. *Margaret Bourke-White: Photographing the World*. New York: Dillon Press, 1992.

Katz, William Loren. *World War II to the New Frontier, 1940-1963*. Austin, Tex.: Raintree Steck-Vaughn, 1993.

Reynoldson, Fiona. *Women and War*. New York: Thomson Learning, 1993.

Smith, Elizabeth Simpson. *Coming Out Right: The Story of Jacqueline Cochran, the First Woman Aviator to Break the Sound Barrier*. New York: Walker, 1991.

Stevens, Bryna. *Deborah Sampson Goes to War*. Minneapolis: Carolrhoda Books, 1984.

Thomas, Gill. *Life on All Fronts: Women in the First World War*. New York: Cambridge University Press, 1989.

Whitman, Sylvia. *Uncle Sam Wants You!: Military Men and Women of World War II*. Minneapolis: Lerner Publications Co., 1993.

Wright, David K. *A Multicultural Portrait of World War II*. New York: Marshall Cavendish, 1994.

INDEX

ABOUT THE AUTHOR

Madelyn Klein Anderson is a graduate of Hunter College, New York University, and Pratt Institute. She is a registered occupational therapist and has a master's degree in library science. She is a former Army officer (post–Korean War) and senior editor of books for young people at a major publishing house. At present she is a consultant in the Office of Educational Research at the Board of Education of the City of New York and is writing her sixteenth book.